I do not know much about gods; but I think that the river

Is a strong brown god—sullen, untamed and intractable,

Patient to some degree, at first recognised as a frontier;

Useful, untrustworthy, as a conveyor of commerce;

Then only a problem confronting the builder of bridges.

The problem once solved, the brown god is almost forgotten

By the dwellers in cities—ever, however, implacable,

Keeping his seasons and rages, destroyer, reminder

Of what men choose to forget. Unhonoured, unpropitiated

By worshippers of the machine, but waiting, watching and waiting.

His rhythm was present in the nursery bedroom,

In the rank ailanthus of the April dooryard,

In the smell of grapes on the autumn table,

And the evening circle in the winter gaslight.

The river is within us....

T. S. ELIOT, *THE DRY SALVAGES*

Excerpt from "The Dry Salvages" in FOUR QUARTETS, copyright 1943 by T.S. Eliot; renewed 1971 by Esme Valerie Eliot. Reprinted by permission of Harcourt Brace Jovanovich, Inc. Excerpt reprinted by permission of the Publishers, The Arthur H. Clark Company, from OLD TIMES ON THE UPPER MISSISSIPPI, by George Byron Merrick. Excerpt reprinted from FLOWING SOUTH by Clark B. Firestone, copyright ©1941 by Robert M. McBride & Company. Used by permission of Crown Publishers, Inc. F. Scott Fitzgerald, excerpted from "Absolution" in ALL THE SAD YOUNG MEN. Copyright 1924 American Mercury, Inc.; copyright renewed 1952 Frances Scott Fitzgerald Lanahan. Reprinted with the permission of Charles Scribner's Sons. Excerpt reprinted from THE CONFIDENCE MAN by Herman Melville, Northwestern University Press Newberry Edition of THE WRITINGS OF HERMAN MELVILLE, 1984. Excerpt from "Jim Smiley and His Jumping Frog" in THE WORKS OF MARK TWAIN, EARLY TALES & SKETCHES, Vol. 2, University of California Press, 1981. Used by permission of the University of California Press. Excerpt from FATHER OF THE BLUES—an Autobiography by W.C. Handy. Reprinted by permission of the Copyright owners, Estate of W.C. Handy. Published by Da Capo Press, Inc., New York, NY 1985. Excerpts from LANTERNS ON THE LEVEE, by William A. Percy. Copyright 1941 by Alfred A. Knopf, Inc. and renewed 1969 by LeRoy Pratt Percy. Reprinted by permission of the publisher. Excerpt from "The Wide Net," copyright 1942, 1970 by Eudora Welty. Reprinted

from her volume THE WIDE NET AND OTHER STORIES by permission of Harcourt Brace Jovanovich, Inc. Excerpts from THE WILD PALMS, by William Faulkner. Copyright 1939 and renewed 1967 by Mrs. William Faulkner and Mrs. Paul D. Summers. Reprinted by permission of Random House, Inc. Excerpt from FATHER ABRAHAM, by William Faulkner, edited by James B. Meriwether. Copyright ©1983 by Jill Faulkner Summers. Reprinted by permission of Random House, Inc. Excerpt from DELTA WEDDING, copyright 1945, 1946, 1973, 1974 by Eudora Welty. Reprinted by permission of Harcourt Brace Jovanovich, Inc. Excerpt from AUDUBON'S AMERICA edited by Donald Culross Peattie. Copyright 1940 and copyright © renewed 1968 by Louise Redfield Peattie. Reprinted by permission of Houghton Mifflin Company. Excerpt from TOW-BOAT RIVER, copyright 1948 by Edwin and Louise Rosskam. A Hawthorn book. Reprinted by permission of E.P. Dutton, a division of New American Library. Excerpt from "Powerhouse," copyright 1941, 1969 by Eudora Welty. Reprinted from her volume A CURTAIN OF GREEN AND OTHER STORIES by permission of Harcourt Brace Jovanovich, Inc.

The publisher has made a thorough effort to locate all persons having any rights or interests in material, and to clear reprint permissions. If any required acknowledgments have been omitted or any rights overlooked, we regret the error.

Lake Itasca, Minnesota, headwaters of Mississippi River

Library of Congress catalog number 85-080973
ISBN 0-934738-13-0
Printed and bound in Japan by Dai Nippon Printing Co., Ltd.
Any inquiries should be directed to the publisher, Thomasson, Grant & Howell, Inc.,
505 Faulconer Drive, Suite 1C, Charlottesville, Virginia 22901.
Compiled and edited by Ross A. Howell, Jr. and Carolyn M. Clark.
Designed by John F. Grant and Marilyn F. Appleby.
Produced by Frank L. Thomasson, III.

THOMASSON, GRANT & HOWELL

(Pages 2-3, overleaf) Tow and barges, Alton, Illinois

GOD OF THE COUNTRY

A Voyage on the Mississippi River

PHOTOGRAPHY BY NATHAN BENN

SELECTIONS FROM AMERICAN LITERATURE

Europen explorers who first saw the Mississippi River 400 years ago were awed by the volume of its waters. The great river was a symbol large enough to encompass the aspirations of a New World. But those explorers could not perceive the full extent of its waters. Forty tributaries that span the continent from Canada to the Gulf of Mexico flow into the Mississippi River, which on the average discharges 453,000 cubic feet of water per second into the sea. Most of the tributaries are navigable, forming an inland waterway system 15,000 miles long.

The river soon embodied the dreams of a new nation. In the 18th century a young Virginian declared that the "Missisipi will be one of the principal channels of commerce for the country westward of the Alleghaney." Years later, President Thomas Jefferson affirmed his statement by purchasing the Louisiana Territory and dispatching the expedition of Meriwether Lewis and William Clark. The river represented the near borders of the wilderness—beyond it lay the American West.

In 19th century America, the Mississippi River steamboat became synonymous with a burgeoning industrial and commercial age. The character of the river—its meanders, its habit of moving its bed without notice, its raging floods—was a source of national pride. "I tell you the United States is a great country!" wrote one chronicler. "There ain't nobody but Uncle Sam as could afford such a river as that! Where *in* airth so much water comes from I can't think!" The "vast solitude" of the river noted by Chateaubriand, the legendary keelboatman Mike Fink, "half wild horse and half cock-eyed alligator," the courage and perseverance of homesteaders, the glorious era of the riverboat pilot, and the freedom of Mark Twain's Huckleberry Finn and Jim on their raft are an enduring part of the American imagination.

For people who have lived within the influence of the Mississippi, for the cities and towns along its banks, for the farms and industries that have been confounded by its floods, the presence of the river is something that goes far beyond geographical data, historical information, or literary tradition. The river is primal. T.S. Eliot, who grew up in St. Louis, called the river a "strong brown god." William Percy, writing of his native Delta, said the river was the "unappeasable god of the country."

Yet few of our national icons have been so maligned. Its floods, color, and smell have earned the Mississippi names like "Ol' Devil River," "Slimy Monster," and most ignominious of all, "The Great Sewer."

"The Mississippi River is not a pretty river," says photographer Nathan Benn, who over the span of a decade worked to capture the significance of the river with his camera. "Compared to the really picturesque rivers of the world, its waters are much too brown and its topography is much too flat. As you travel on the surface of the Mississippi, the scenery is generally obscured by levees, which are generally of uniform height, and the levees are covered with scrubby trees. It gets monotonous. You could be passing a town of 50,000 people, and all you might see is a bank cupola and a church steeple—the only hints that there is a town on the other side of the levee. And yet the river is very beautiful, if you come to understand it in its larger sense."

It was not the river as a subject that first drew Benn to the Mississippi. "Back in 1973, I started working on a book on rural America," he says. "It was important to me that the book not be blind to the fact that much of rural America is poor. I did some research on where I might go to photograph rural poverty. That led me to Mississippi, the poorest state in the nation. When I was there, I went to hear Robert Coles, who was lecturing in Jackson. His sociological studies of sharecroppers had made a great impression on me. I told him about my project. He sent me to Bolivar County, the poorest county in Mississippi at the time. There I found Beulah, one of the poorest towns in Bolivar County. It stands right on the levee of the Mississippi River. So my first contact with the river came not because I was looking for it, but because I was looking for sharecroppers. The people of Beulah don't have a sense of the river by reading William Faulkner. They live those novels."

The people of Beulah, and the unique character of the river itself, drew Benn back on a series of assignments. "I always had the sense that I was photographing a river of mythic proportions. There are many children who grow up reading Mark Twain and dream of floating down the river on a raft. I didn't. I read only a little Twain and never dreamed of traveling on the river. I had grown up in Florida and had never been off the East Coast.

"Everything about the river was fresh and new to me. It was exotic, like being in a foreign country. You cannot travel along the river and not be aware of the literature that is associated with it. The river is so big, there are so many towns and cities along its banks, it has so many changes of character, that the literature becomes one of the bases for directing your work. I tried to figure out why I was in a specific location, what symbols or themes the place might embody. Was I there because the place was important for its river traffic? For its agriculture? Music? Industry? Plantations? There were times when I would see the contours of farmland in Wisconsin, or shacks scattered along a dusty street in Arkansas, and those scenes would act like visual cues reminding me of all the symbols, the iconography of our country."

Along the river's 2,350-mile reach, Benn found images of America's history. "When you start at the headwaters of the Mississippi," he says, "you find native Americans food-gathering, harvesting wild rice. The source of the river still reminds us in a metaphorical way of our origins as a nation. And among the Chippewas there is a strong revival of a sense of community and their identity as a people. Their dances, or pow-wows, were very popular, from the youngest children to very old people, as sources of pride and identity. This ancient tradition was something that had almost died out."

In times of modern agribusiness and massive equipment, Benn saw evidence of the ideals of 19th century homesteaders whose fields served as the "breadbasket of democracy." "One of the things that becomes apparent right away as you travel on the river is that it serves as a grain conduit for the world," says Benn. "The giant grain elevators, the lushness, and richness, and abundance of the land are very obvious. Grant Wood's paintings seem quite realistic after you see the Iowa countryside. The land really does contour that way. The barns really are that color. And you don't have to look hard to find evidence of traditional small-town values. Hard work. Honesty. Caring for your neighbor. A town like Winona, Minnesota, made me feel good about my country in a very sappy sort of way. I could walk down to the town park on any weekday afternoon after school and watch six or eight Little League baseball games."

The spirit of the town where one of our country's favorite writers spent his boyhood over a century ago is still palpable. "Hannibal, Missouri, stands right by the levee," says Benn. "In many ways, it is still the town where young Samuel Clemens grew up. Of course, there's the tourism that results from the popularity of Mark Twain. But Hannibal is still an agricultural town. It supplies the farmers in the region with the goods and clothing that they need. When the farmers sell grain, it goes to the elevators along the riverfront in Hannibal, is loaded in barges and goes down the river. That's fundamentally the town that Mark Twain knew."

The river continues to offer the challenge and serenity that attracted Twain as a cub pilot. "I rode on a barge carrying industrial molasses from St. Paul, Minnesota, to the Quad Cities of Iowa and Illinois," says Benn. "I'd never dreamed there was such a thing as industrial molasses, much less that seven grown people would be taking a multimillion-dollar barge down the river carrying the stuff, which is used in cattle feeds. The pace on a barge is very slow. I had five days to smell the generous odor of our cargo. There was a six-man crew, including the captain, and a big woman who was the cook. The first mate was a guy named Buddy, who wrote poetry, fished, and carved. We ran 24 hours a day. Even with modern navigational aids, it was amazing to see a captain running the river at night. Pilots committing the shape of the river to memory—that hasn't changed from Mark Twain's day. Tow captains today know the river as well as the steamboat captains of 150 years ago, and they are just as capable at the controls. Barges are almost impossible to stop because of the mass involved. And it's an excruciatingly long process to take a large number of barges through a lock. The barges must be broken into two or three sections, then secured back to the tow after the lock is cleared. The pace is the old riverboat pace."

And Benn saw vestiges of the Old South that Twain often lambasted. "You don't have *Gone With the Wind* plantation life in grand mansions the way it used to be. But there are remnants of the genteel society familiar to many of us through the literature of the Old South. In Natchez, Mississippi, there are still grand old properties, and many of the people who inherited those houses carry on the lifestyle we tend to associate with them. And the Garden District in New

Orleans is very beautiful and impressive. There you still see tea dances on Sunday afternoon. It's a very social, very genteel, very comfortable place."

In his journeys along the river, Benn also came across the soulful product of the Mississippi, its music. The Delta offered the blues. "I spent a good deal of time in Wade Walton's Barber Shop in Clarksippi," he says. "Wade is first generation, one of the originators of the blues form. He did an album, although it's probably not available in your local record shop. Blues musicians receive more recognition in Europe, especially Germany and France, than in the United States. Twice I was in the shop when young European kids, hitchhiking around the country, had managed to track Wade down. They came in—they just wanted to see him. Wade played electric guitar and harmonica. He kept the instruments in his shop. When he felt like it, he would stop cutting hair and start playing. His wife ran a little bar in the back of the barber shop. There were some tables and a juke box. It was a pleasant neighborhood tap room."

The streets of New Orleans offered jazz. "I met Preston Jackson, a trombone player, when I wanted to photograph musicians away from Preservation Hall," says Benn. "I didn't know where they got together to jam, and one of the managers of the Hall said he would arrange for me to photograph some of the musicians at home. Preston Jackson lived by himself in two or three very small rooms behind a large house in the French Quarter. His rooms were very, very simple. He told me he had played with Louis Armstrong in his early days."

The many vignettes from the river's past have particular relevance today. "All along the river during the time I was photographing, people were seeking their roots and the roots of their communities," says Benn. "Many of the river towns had been built in the 18th and 19th centuries in response to keelboat or steamboat traffic. Consequently, their business centers sat right beside the levees. In the 20th century, many towns and cities moved away from intimate contact with the river after rails, trucks, and airplanes became more important means of transportation than the river traffic.

"People also screened themselves from the river because they feared its floods. I remember seeing towns where massive concrete walls, maybe 15 or 20 feet tall and three feet thick, were built along the levee. You could live in a Mississippi River town and never know that a river was even near it. Ironically, many of the downtowns where these walls had been built were completely deserted. They were so afraid of being flooded that they killed themselves."

But Benn saw cities and towns reclaiming the river as a source of identity and definition. "I could sense a revival of awareness of the river and of local traditions," says Benn. "Every town seems to have a river festival now. Waterfront commercial districts that were once derelict have been renovated into beautiful residential and entertainment areas. St. Louis, Natchez, Memphis, New Orleans, and many other cities and towns have made improvements on their waterfronts. The river is an organic part of the lives of people who live in those towns again."

To a degree the river is a part of the life of each American. "As I continued photographing the river," says Benn, "I began to realize that if you worked, scratched around, the river could give you a sense of where we've come from as a people and as a country. The river is so long, covers so much territory, and is so diverse. It touches on so many themes about life."

The diversity of Benn's experience in photographing the Mississippi suggests the significance of the river itself. The Mississippi's changing moods, its restless wandering, and its dramatic changes in climate remind us of our history and diversity as a nation. Within its influence some of our greatest writers were born and raised, and within its influence art forms we call American took root and flourished. Symbol for a New World, large as the Great West, spine of transport for a nation, mighty and inscrutable as a deity, this powerful, homely, and muddy god is one of the sources of American identity.

Washington, D.C. and Charlottesville, Virginia
May 1985

THE MISSISSIPPI RIVER

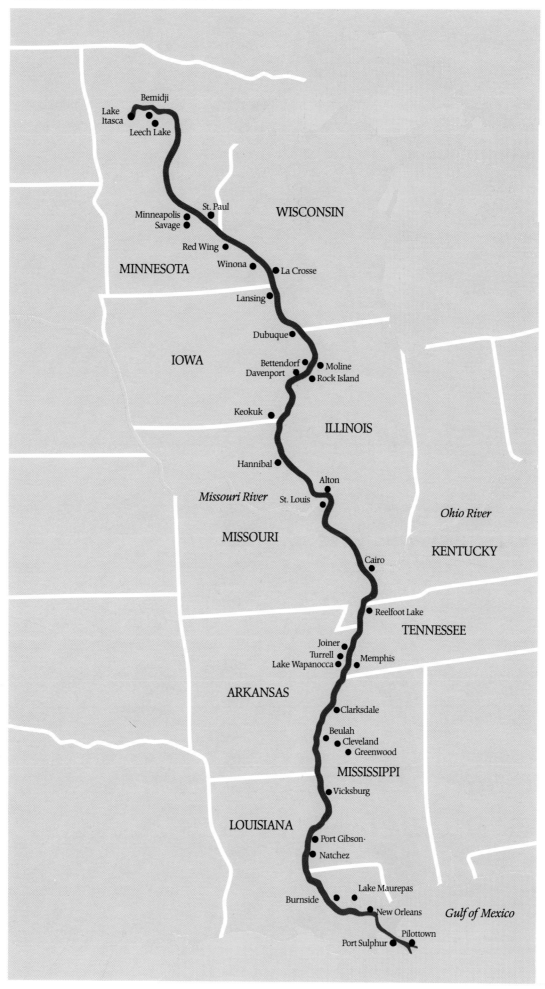

Bemidji

Lake Itasca

Leech Lake

WISCONSIN

MINNEAPOLIS
Savage

St. Paul

MINNESOTA

Red Wing

Winona

La Crosse

Lansing

Dubuque

IOWA

Bettendorf
Davenport

Moline
Rock Island

Keokuk

ILLINOIS

Hannibal

Alton

Missouri River

St. Louis

Ohio River

MISSOURI

KENTUCKY

Cairo

Reelfoot Lake

TENNESSEE

Joiner
Turrell
Lake Wapanocca

Memphis

ARKANSAS

Clarksdale

Beulah
Cleveland
Greenwood

MISSISSIPPI

Vicksburg

LOUISIANA

Port Gibson·
Natchez

Lake Maurepas

Burnside

New Orleans

Gulf of Mexico

Pilottown
Port Sulphur

12 *Mississippi River near Bemidji, Minnesota*

Chippewa dancer at "pow-wow," Minnesota

THE CHIPPEWAS called their river Mee-zee-see-bee, Father of Waters. Like many of their phrases, this is strong poetry, and though they are a dwindling and almost forgotten people, the name still carries the spell that a great river cast upon the mind of a primitive race. To them the river was one of the lordly and living features of the earth. It was a boundary, a landmark, a highway, a path of light and movement through their ancestral wilderness.

WALTER HAVIGHURST, *UPPER MISSISSIPPI*

Gathering wild rice, Leech Lake, Minnesota

Chippewa boy, Minnesota

FOR THE DANCE ITSELF a large open space was selected along the river, so that the camp fires and torches threw their reflections on the water. The Indian drummers squatted on the ground in a circle, playing their tomtoms. Inside the circle were the performers, who danced with a kind of frenzy.

One of the first Indian dances I ever saw took place on a river bend, against a background of tall timber and deep shadows. Coming down river on a steamboat one night, we noticed a glare in the sky some distance away. It increased in intensity as we drew nearer, until we were full upon it and saw silhouetted against its brilliance the dark forms of the Indians, dancing rhythmically to the beating of the tomtoms. We ran as close to the shore and as slowly as possible so that all on board might witness that colorful pageant. As long as I live I shall never forget the weird beauty of those fantastic figures leaping in the firelight.

CAPTAIN FRANK J. FUGINA, *LORE AND LURE OF THE UPPER MISSISSIPPI RIVER*

THE SEASON ON THE UPPER RIVER is short at best. An early start in the spring, before the railroads had yet reached St. Paul, brought the greatest financial returns to the daring and successful captains who, bringing their boats through all the dangers, arrived safely in harbor at the head of navigation. Great chances were taken in the fifties, in trying to get through Lake Pepin before it was clear of ice. The river above and below was usually clear two weeks before the ice was out of the lake sufficiently to enable a boat to force its way through. During the last week of such embargo, boats were constantly butting the ice at either end of the lake, trying to get up or down, or were perilously coasting along the shore, where, from the shallowness of the water and the inflow from the banks, the ice had rotted more than in the centre of the lake. A change of wind, or a sudden freshening, catching a boat thus coasting along the shore, would shove her on to the rocks or sand, and crush her hull as though it were an eggshell. The "Falls City" was thus caught and smashed. I myself saw the "Fire Canoe" crushed flat, in the middle of the lake, a little below Wacouta, Minn., she having run down a mile or more in the channel which we had broken with the "Fanny Harris." We had just backed out, for Captain Anderson had seen signs of a rising wind out of the west, that would shut the ice into our track. This result did follow after the other boat had gone in, despite the well-meant warnings of Anderson, who hailed the other boat and warned them of the rising wind and the danger to be apprehended. This caution was ignored by the "Fire Canoe's" captain, who ran his boat down into the channel that we had broken. The ice did move as predicted, slowly, so slowly as to be imperceptible unless you sighted by some stationary object. But it was as irresistible as fate, and it crushed the timbers of the "Fire Canoe" as though they were inch boards instead of five-inch planks.

GEORGE BYRON MERRICK, *OLD TIMES ON THE UPPER MISSISSIPPI*

Tow breaking ice near St. Paul, Minnesota

(Pages 18-19, overleaf) Tow and oil barges, Alton, Illinois

(Above and facing) Freshwater clam harvest, Wisconsin

NOW AND THEN I SAW SMALL MUSSEL BOATS moving along the Mississippi's shore or coming out of one of its tributaries. They were flat-bottomed, each with a rack over it on which were hung two iron bars with a hundred or more stout crowfoot hooks suspended by short trot-lines. Mussels lie in the mud or gravel of the river's bottom with their valves slightly open; they close them tightly when a hook enters, and are brought to the surface. So in a sense this industry goes on out of sight, seems obscure, and in fact is little remarked upon. Yet it is important, because every man who has half a dozen shirts and half a dozen suits of underwear in his bureau drawers uses at least a hundred pearl buttons a year. These were once the shells of fresh-water mussels.

The fishery is called clamming, or shelling. It is almost a monopoly of the Mississippi and its affluents. Mussel shells in the rivers draining to the Atlantic can be used only for lime stucco, poultry grit, and road metal. Those in the Mississippi Valley are worked up into buttons which have the luster of pearls.

CLARK B. FIRESTONE, *FLOWING SOUTH*

Senior eight-man shell, Minnesota Boat Club, St. Paul, Minnesota

Minnehapolis, Opposite St. Anthony, November 5, 1852

Mr. Bowman:

We are accustomed, on this side of the river, to regard your paper as a sort of exponent of public sentiment, and as a proper medium of public expression—

My purpose, in this communication, is to suggest a remedy for the anomalous position we occupy of dwelling in the place selected by the constituted authorities of Hennepin county as the county seat; which as yet bears no name, unless the miserable misnomer, All Saints, shall be considered so thrust upon us that the unanimous determination of the inhabitants cannot throw it off—It is a name that is applicable to no more than two persons in the vicinity of the falls, and of doubtful application even to them.

The name I propose, Minnehapolis, derived from Minnehaha (laughing water) with the Greek affix, polis (a city), meaning "Laughing Water City," or "City of the Falls"— you perceive I spell it with an "h," which is silent in the pronunciation.

This name has been favorably received by many of the inhabitants to whom it has been proposed, and unless a better can be suggested it is hoped this effort to christen our place will not prove abortive as those heretofore named. I am aware that other names have been proposed, such as Lowell, Brooklyn, Addiesville, etc., but until some one is decided upon we intend to call ourselves Minnehapolis.

Charles Hoag

LETTER TO THE EDITOR, *ST. ANTHONY EXPRESS*

Farm near La Crosse, Wisconsin

   OUTSIDE THE WINDOW the blue sirocco trembled over the wheat, and girls with yellow hair walked sensuously along roads that bounded the fields, calling innocent, exciting things to the young men who were working in the lines between the grain. Legs were shaped under starchless gingham, and rims of the necks of dresses were warm and damp. For five hours now hot fertile life had burned in the afternoon. It would be night in three hours, and all along the land there would be these blonde Northern girls and the tall young men from the farms lying out beside the wheat, under the moon.

—F. SCOTT FITZGERALD, *ABSOLUTION*

Meat-packing house, Dubuque, Iowa

THE MISSISSIPPI! How, as by an enchanted wand, have its scenes been changed, since Chateaubriand wrote his prose-poetic description of it, as a river of mighty, un-broken solitudes, rolling amid undreamed wonders of vegetable and animal existence.

But, as in an hour, this river of dreams and wild romance has emerged to a reality scarcely less visionary and splendid. What other river of the world bears on its bosom to the ocean the wealth and enterprise of such another country?—a country whose products embrace all between the tropics and the poles! Those turbid waters, hurrying, foaming, tearing along, an apt resemblance of that headlong tide of business which is poured along its wave by a race more vehement and energetic than any the world ever saw.

HARRIET BEECHER STOWE, *UNCLE TOM'S CABIN*

(Above) Wheat samples and trading "pit," Minneapolis Grain Exchange, Minnesota

(Pages 28-29, overleaf) Thunderstorm near Savage, Minnesota

AS THE WORD ABRAHAM means the father of a great multitude of men, so the word Mississippi means the father of a great multitude of waters. His tribes stream in from east and west, exceedingly fruitful the lands they enrich. In this granary of a continent, this basin of the Mississippi, will not the nations be greatly multiplied and blest?

—HERMAN MELVILLE

(Above and facing) Grain-loading facilities, Savage, Minnesota

Railroad tank car near Vicksburg, Mississippi

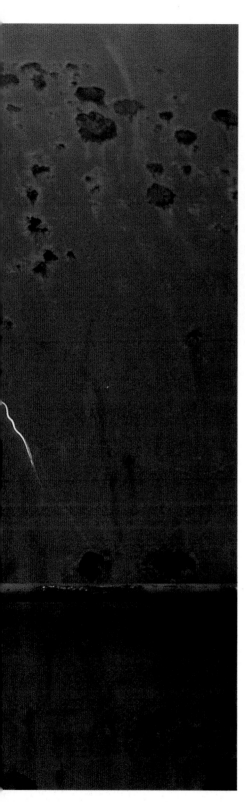

Dock near Savage, Minnesota

PIERRE PAUQUETTE lived opposite Fort Winnebago on what was called the Agency Hill. He was a half-breed Winnebago Indian and French trader, who kept fifteen or twenty yoke of oxen to haul goods across the portage. He was born at St. Louis, Missouri, in 1876, and engaged in the Indian trade at an early day. He was a fine specimen of manhood—six feet, two inches in height, large, and very heavy. He was handsome and good natured. His flesh was hard and is said to have been more like bone than like muscle. His thigh was as large around as an ordinary person's waist. He was extraordinarily strong. He could pick up a barrel of pork and throw it into a wagon as easily as a ten gallon keg. He once lifted off the ground a cask with eight hundred pounds of white lead in it. At one time, the story is told that, as he was hauling a boat across the portage with ox teams, one of the oxen gave out and would not pull. Pauquette took off the bow, pulled the ox to one side, and taking hold of the yoke, pulled beside the other ox.

SUSAN BURDICK DAVIS, *OLD FORTS AND REAL FOLKS*

Mixing tank, Winona, Minnesota

WHILE HIS DIVING-BELL BOAT was building, a barge loaded with pig-lead sank in the rapids at Keokuk, 212 miles from St. Louis. A contract having been made with its owners, Eads hurried up there to rescue the freight from fifteen feet of water. He had no knowledge himself of diving-armor; but he had engaged a skilled diver from the Great Lakes, who brought his own apparatus. They set out in a barge and anchored over the wreck; but, once there, they soon discovered that the current was so exceedingly rapid that the diver could do nothing in it. Eads at once returned to Keokuk, and, buying a forty-gallon whisky hogshead, took it out to the wreck; and having knocked out one head, he slung pigs of lead round his improvised diving-bell, made a seat inside it, rigged it to his derrick and air-pumps, and then asked the diver to go down in it. The diver having very naturally refused, Eads on the spot set himself a precedent which, during his after life, he never broke—saying that he would not ask an employee to go where he would not trust himself, he got inside his hogshead and was lowered into the river. His assistants were unused to managing diving-bells, and, when they came to haul him up, the derrick got out of order. By main force they were able to raise the hogshead to the surface, but not above it. As the air-pump continued to work all the while, Eads, though wondering what was amiss, sat patiently in his place till finally he saw a hand appear under the rim of the hogshead. Seizing this, he ducked under and got out. Although the rough diving-bell worked thus awkwardly at first, it served well enough, and finally all of the lost freight was saved.

LOUIS HOW, *JAMES B. EADS*

Generator foundations, hydroelectric plant, Keokuk, Iowa

(Pages 36-37, overleaf) Old Lock #26, Alton, Illinois

Barge, St. Paul, Minnesota

THE MILITARY ENGINEERS of the Commission have taken upon their shoulders the job of making the Mississippi over again—a job transcended in size by only the original job of creating it. They are building wing-dams here and there to deflect the current; and dikes to confine it in narrower bounds; and other dikes to make it stay there; and for unnumbered miles along the Mississippi they are felling the timber-front for fifty yards back, with the purpose of shaving the bank down to low-water mark with the slant of a house-roof, and ballasting it with stones; and in many places they have protected the wasting shores with rows of piles. One who knows the Mississippi will promptly aver—not aloud but to himself—that ten thousand River Commissions, with the mines of the world at their back, cannot tame that lawless stream, cannot curb it or confine it, cannot say to it, "Go here," or "Go there," and make it obey; cannot save a shore which it has sentenced; cannot bar its path with an obstruction which it will not tear down, dance over, and laugh at. But a discreet man will not put these things into spoken words; for the West Point engineers have not their superiors anywhere; they know all that can be known of their abstruse science; and so, since they conceive that they can fetter and handcuff that river and boss him, it is but wisdom for the unscientific man to keep still, lie low, and wait till they do it.

MARK TWAIN, *LIFE ON THE MISSISSIPPI*

New lock construction, Army Corps of Engineers, Alton, Illinois

TWO OR THREE DAYS AND NIGHTS WENT BY; I reckon I might say they swum by, they slid along so quiet and smooth and lovely. Here is the way we put in the time. It was a monstrous big river down there—sometimes a mile and a half wide; we run nights, and laid up and hid day-times; soon as night was most gone, we stopped navigating and tied up—nearly always in the dead water under a tow-head; and then cut young cottonwoods and willows and hid the raft with them. Then we set out the lines. Next we slid into the river and had a swim, so as to freshen up and cool off; then we set down on the sandy bottom where the water was about knee deep, and watched the daylight come. Not a sound, anywheres—perfectly still—just like the whole world was asleep, only sometimes the bull-frogs a-cluttering, maybe. The first thing to see, looking away over the water, was a kind of dull line—that was the woods on t'other side—you couldn't make nothing else out; then a pale place in the sky; then more paleness, spreading around; then the river softened up, away off, and warn't black any more, but gray; you could see little dark spots drifting along, ever so far away—trading scows, and such things; and long black streaks—rafts; sometimes you could hear a sweep screaking; or jumbled up voices, it was so still, and sounds come so far; and by-and-by you could see a streak on the water which you know by the look of the streak that there's a snag there in a swift current which breaks on it and makes that streak look that way; and you see the mist curl up off of the water, and the east reddens up, and the river, and you make out a log cabin in the edge of the woods, away on the bank on t'other side of the river, being a wood-yard, likely, and piled by them cheats so you can throw a dog through it anywheres; then the nice breeze springs up, and comes fanning you from over there, so cool and fresh, and sweet to smell, on account of the woods and the flowers; but sometimes not that way, because they've left dead fish laying around, gars, and such, and they do get pretty rank; and next you've got the full day, and everything smiling in the sun, and the song-birds just going it!

MARK TWAIN, *THE ADVENTURES OF HUCKLEBERRY FINN*

Dubuque, Iowa

Paddlewheel of Mississippi Queen, near Vicksburg, Mississippi

I WENT TO WORK now to learn the shape of the river; and of all the eluding and ungraspable objects that ever I tried to get mind or hands on, that was the chief. I would fasten my eyes upon a sharp, wooded point that projected far into the river some miles ahead of me, and go to laboriously photographing its shape upon my brain; and just as I was beginning to succeed to my satisfaction, we would draw up toward it and the exasperating thing would begin to melt away and fold back into the bank! If there had been a conspicuous dead tree standing upon the very point of the cape, I would find that tree inconspicuously merged into the general forest, and occupying the middle of a straight shore, when I got abreast of it! No prominent hill would stick to its shape long enough for me to make up my mind what its form really was, but it was as dissolving and changeful as if it had been a mountain of butter in the hottest corner of the tropics. Nothing ever had the same shape when I was coming downstream that it had borne when I went up. I mentioned these little difficulties to Mr. Bixby. He said:

"That's the main virtue of the thing. If the shapes didn't change every three seconds they wouldn't be of any use. Take this place where we are now, for instance. As long as that hill over yonder is only one hill, I can boom right along the way I'm going; but the moment it splits at the top and forms a V, I know I've got to scratch to starboard in a hurry, or I'll bang this boat's brains out against a rock; and then the moment one of the prongs of the V swings behind the other, I've got to waltz to larboard again, or I'll have a misunderstanding with a snag that would snatch the keelson out of this steamboat as neatly as if it were a sliver in your hand. If that hill didn't change its shape on bad nights there would be an awful steamboat graveyard around here inside of a year."

It was plain that I had got to learn the shape of the river in all the different ways that could be thought of—upside down, wrong end first, inside out, fore-and-aft, and "thort-ships"—and then know what to do on gray nights when it hadn't any shape at all. So I set about it. In the course of time I began to get the best of this knotty lesson, and my self-complacency moved to the front once more. Mr. Bixby was all fixed, and ready to start it to the rear again. He opened on me after this fashion:

"How much water did we have in the middle crossing at Hole-in-the-Wall, trip before last?"

I considered this an outrage. I said:

"Every trip down and up, the leadsmen are singing through that tangled place for three-quarters of an hour on a stretch. How do you reckon I can remember such a mess as that?"

"My boy, you've got to remember it. You've got to remember the exact spot and the exact marks the boat lay in when we had the shoalest water, in every one of the five hundred shoal places between St. Louis and New Orleans; and you mustn't get the shoal soundings and marks of one trip mixed up with the shoal soundings and marks of another, either, for they're not often twice alike. You must keep them separate."

When I came to myself again, I said:

"When I get so that I can do that, I'll be able to raise the dead, and then I won't have to pilot a steamboat to make a living. I want to retire from this business. I want a slush-bucket and a brush; I'm only fit for a roustabout. I haven't got brains enough to be a pilot; and if I had I wouldn't have strength enough to carry them around, unless I went on crutches."

"Now drop that! When I say I'll learn a man the river, I mean it. And you can depend on it, I'll learn him or kill him."

MARK TWAIN, *LIFE ON THE MISSISSIPPI*

Catfish from Mississippi River, Joiner, Arkansas

(Pages 44-45, overleaf) Delta Queen, near Memphis, Tennessee

THEN THEY GOT TO TALKING about differences betwixt hogs, and their different kind of habits; and next about women and their different ways; and next about the best way to put out houses that was afire; and next about what ought to be done with the Injuns; and next about what a king had to do, and how much he got; and next about how to make cats fight; and next about what to do when a man has fits; and next about differences betwixt clear-water rivers and muddy-water ones. The man they called Ed said the muddy Mississippi water was wholesomer to drink than the clear water of the Ohio; he said if you let a pint of this yaller Mississippi water settle, you would have about a half to three-quarters of an inch of mud in the bottom, according to the stage of the river, and then it warn't no better than Ohio water —what you wanted to do was to keep it stirred up—and when the river was low, keep mud on hand to put in and thicken the water up the way it ought to be.

MARK TWAIN, *LIFE ON THE MISSISSIPPI*

Ice cream social, Lansing, Iowa

Frog-jumping contest, Hannibal, Missouri

WELL, THISH-YER SMILEY had rat-terriers and chicken cocks, and tom-cats, and all them kind of things, till you couldn't rest, and you couldn't fetch nothing for him to bet on but he'd match you. He ketched a frog one day and took him home and said he cal'lated to educate him; and so he never done nothing for three months but set in his back yard and learn that frog to jump. And you bet you he *did* learn him, too. He'd give him a little hunch behind, and the next minute you'd see that frog whirling in the air like a doughnut—see him turn one summerset, or maybe a couple, if he got a good start, and come down flat-footed and all right, like a cat. He got him up so in the matter of ketching flies, and kept him in practice so constant, that he'd nail a fly every time as far as he could see him. Smiley said all a frog wanted was education, and he could do most anything—and I believe him. Why, I've seen him set Dan'l Webster down here on this floor—Dan'l Webster was the name of the frog—and sing out, "Flies! Dan'l, flies," and quicker'n you could wink, he'd spring straight up, and snake a fly off'n the counter there, and flop down on the floor again as solid as a gob of mud, and fall to scratching the side of his head with his hind foot as indifferent as if he hadn't no idea he'd done any more'n any frog might do. You never see a frog so modest and straightfor'ard as he was, for all he was so gifted. And when it come to fair-and-square jumping on a dead level, he could get over more ground at one straddle than any animal of his breed you ever see.

MARK TWAIN, *JIM SMILEY AND HIS JUMPING FROG*

"SAY—I'M GOING IN A-SWIMMING, I AM. Don't you wish you could? But of course you'd druther *work* wouldn't you? Course you would!"

Tom contemplated the boy a bit, and said:

"What do you call work?"

"Why, ain't *that* work?"

Tom resumed his whitewashing, and answered carelessly:

"Well, maybe it is, and maybe it ain't. All I know, is, it suits Tom Sawyer."

"Oh come, now, you don't mean to let on that you *like* it?"

The brush continued to move.

"Like it? Well, I don't see why I oughtn't to like it. Does a boy get a chance to whitewash a fence every day?"

That put the thing in a new light. Ben stopped nibbling his apple. Tom swept his brush daintily back and forth—stepped back to note the effect—added a touch here and there—criticized the effect again—Ben watching every move and getting more and more interested, more and more absorbed. Presently he said:

"Say, Tom, let *me* whitewash a little."

MARK TWAIN, *THE ADVENTURES OF TOM SAWYER*

(Above and facing) Whitewashing contest and shower after mud volleyball game, Hannibal, Missouri

ONCE A DAY a cheap, gaudy packet arrived upward from St. Louis, and another downward from Keokuk. Before these events, the day was glorious with expectancy; after them, the day was a dead and empty thing. Not only the boys, but the whole village, felt this. After all these years I can picture that old time to myself now, just as it was then: the white town drowsing in the sunshine of a summer's morning; the streets empty, or pretty nearly so; one or two clerks sitting in front of the Water Street stores, with their splint-bottomed chairs tilted back against the walls, chins on breasts, hats slouched over their faces, asleep—with shingle-shavings enough around to show what broke them down; a sow and a litter of pigs loafing along the sidewalk, doing a good business in watermelon rinds and seeds; two or three lonely little freight piles scattered about the "levee"; a pile of "skids" on the slope of the stone-paved wharf, and the fragrant town drunkard asleep in the shadow of them; two or three wood flats at the head of the wharf, but nobody to listen to the peaceful lapping of the wavelets against them; the great Mississippi, the majestic, the magnificent Mississippi, rolling its mile-wide tide along, shining in the sun; the dense forest away on the other side; the "point" above the town, and the "point" below, bounding the river-glimpse and turning it into a sort of sea, and withal a very still and brilliant and lonely one. Presently a film of dark smoke appears above one of those remote "points"; instantly a negro drayman, famous for his quick eye and prodigious voice, lifts up the cry, "S-t-e-a-m-boat a-comin'!" and the scene changes! The town drunkard stirs, the clerks wake up, a furious clatter of drays follows, every house and store pours out a human contribution, and all in a twinkling the dead town is alive and moving. Drays, carts, men, boys, all go hurrying from many quarters to a common center, the wharf. Assembled there, the people fasten their eyes upon the coming boat as upon a wonder they are seeing for the first time.

MARK TWAIN, *LIFE ON THE MISSISSIPPI*

Delta Queen and *Mississippi Queen*, Natchez, Mississippi

(Pages 54-55, overleaf) Confluence of Mississippi River and Ohio River near Cairo, Illinois

(Pages 56-57, overleaf) St. Louis, Missouri

Busch Stadium, St. Louis

OCT., NOV., AND DEC., '79.—The points of St. Louis are its position, its absolute wealth, (the long accumulations of time and trade, solid riches, probably a higher average thereof than any city,) the unrivall'd amplitude of its well-laid out environage of broad plateaus, for future expansion— and the great State of which it is the head. It fuses northern and southern qualities, perhaps native and foreign ones, to perfection, rendezvous the whole stretch of the Mississippi and Missouri rivers, and its American electricity goes well with its German phlegm. Fourth, Fifth and Third streets are store-streets, showy, modern, metropolitan, with hurrying crowds, vehicles, horse-cars, hubbub, plenty of people, rich goods, plate-glass windows, iron fronts often five or six stories high. You can purchase anything in St. Louis (in most of the big western cities for the matter of that) just as readily and cheaply as in the Atlantic marts. Often in going about the town you see reminders of old, even decay'd civilization. The water of the west, in some places, is not good, but they make it up here by plenty of very fair wine, and inexhaustible quantities of the best beer in the world.

WALT WHITMAN, *ST. LOUIS MEMORANDA*

THE GAMES which were mostly played in those days on river steamers were poker, brag, whist, Boston, and old sledge; and if banking games were set up in the social hall, they were usually *vingt-et-un,* chuck, and sometimes faro. According to the rules of these steamers, all gambling was prohibited after ten o'clock in the evening; but in many instances these rules were a dead letter, and the morning sun frequently found one or more parties at the card-table engaged at their favorite games. In these jolly times the steamboat officers mingled with the passengers in the cabin as equals, and it was no uncommon thing to see uncouth pilots, mates, and greasy engineers engaged at the card-tables with well-dressed travelers. Passengers were privileged to amuse themselves just as they pleased, so long as they did not infringe upon the rights of others, or interfere in any respect with the duties of the officers or crew. This latitude sometimes led to some rather strong contrasts; for instance, there might frequently be seen in the ladies' cabin a group of the godly praying and singing psalms, while in the dining-saloon, from which the tables had been removed, another party were dancing merrily to the music of a fiddle, while farther along, in the social hall, might be heard the loud laughter of jolly carousers around the drinking bar, and occasionally chiming in with the sound of the revelry, the rattling of money and checks, and the sound of voices at the card-tables.

JOHN MORRIS (PSEUD. JOHN O'CONNOR), *WANDERINGS OF A VAGABOND*

Natchez, Mississippi

Delta Queen near Cairo, Illinois

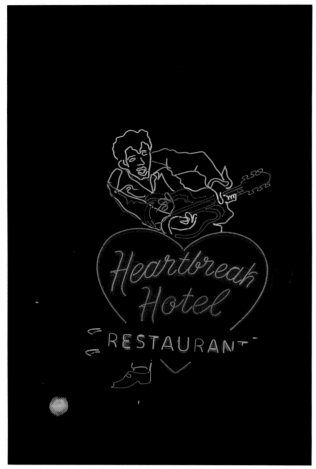

Memphis, Tennessee

I RENTED A ROOM in the Beale Street section and went to work. Outside, the lights flickered. Chitterling joints were as crowded as the more fashionable resorts like the Iroquois. Piano thumpers tickled the ivories in the saloons to attract customers, furnishing a theme for the prayers at Beale Street Baptist Church and Avery Chapel (Methodist). Scores of powerfully built roustabouts from river boats sauntered along the pavement, elbowing fashionable browns in beautiful gowns. Pimps in boxback coats and undented Stetsons came out to get a breath of early evening air and to welcome the young night. The poolhall crowd grew livelier than they had been during the day. All that contributed to the color and spell of Beale Street mingled outside, but I neither saw nor heard it that night. I had a song to write.

W.C. HANDY, *FATHER OF THE BLUES*

Bus to Memphis, Cleveland, Mississippi

Clarksdale, Mississippi

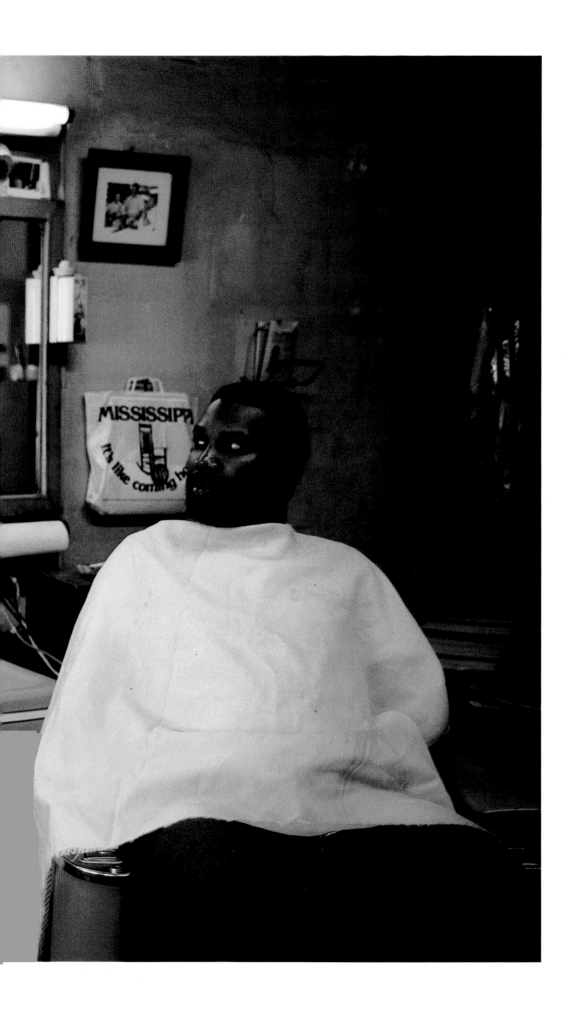

Flooded chicken coop near Vicksburg, Mississippi

THE 1927 FLOOD was a torrent ten feet deep the size of Rhode Island; it was thirty-six hours coming and four months going; it was deep enough to drown a man, swift enough to upset a boat, and lasting enough to cancel a crop year. The only islands in it were eight or ten tiny Indian mounds and the narrow spoil-banks of a few drainage canals. Between the torrent and the river ran the levee, dry on the land side and on the top. The south Delta became seventy-five hundred square miles of mill-race in which one hundred and twenty thousand human beings and one hundred thousand animals squirmed and bobbed.

In the thirty-six hours which the river required after its victory at Scott to submerge the country, panicky people poured out of Greenville by the last trains and by automobiles over roads axle-deep in water. These were mostly frantic mothers with their children, non-residents from the hills who regarded the river hysterically and not devotedly, and the usual run of rabbit folk who absent themselves in every emergency. During the same hours of grace panicky people poured into Greenville. These were mostly Negroes in dilapidated Fords, on the running-boards of trucks, or afoot carrying babies, leading children, and pulling cows, who are always at their worst in crises. Outside of town stock was being rushed cross-country to the levee, and Negroes were being piled into lofts, gins, and compresses by plantation managers. For thirty-six hours the Delta was in turmoil, in movement, in terror. Then the waters covered everything, the turmoil ceased, and a great quiet settled down; the stock which had not reached the levee had been drowned; the owners of second-story houses with their pantries and kitchens had moved upstairs; those in one-story houses had taken to the roofs and the trees. Over everything was silence, deadlier because of the strange cold sound of the currents gnawing at foundations, hissing against walls, creaming and clawing over obstructions.

WILLIAM A. PERCY, *LANTERNS ON THE LEVEE*

THEN THE LIGHT CHANGED THE WATER, until all about them the woods in the rising wind seemed to grow taller and blow inward together and suddenly turn dark. The rain struck heavily. A huge tail seemed to lash through the air and the river broke in a wound of silver. In silence the party crouched and stooped beside the trunk of the great tree, which in the push of the storm rose full of a fragrance and unyielding weight. Where they all stared, past their tree, was another tree, and beyond that another and another, all the way down the bank of the river, all towering and darkened in the storm.

"The outside world is full of endurance," said Doc. "Full of endurance."

EUDORA WELTY, *THE WIDE NET*

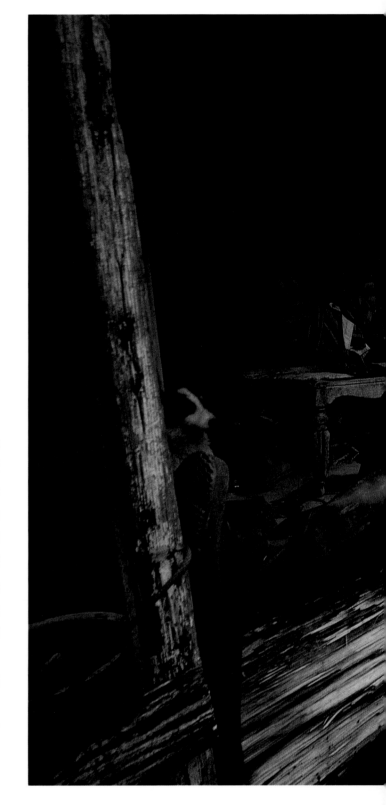

Near Vicksburg, Mississippi

(Pages 68-69, overleaf) Greenwood, Mississippi

Cairo, Illinois

THEN THE TALLER CONVICT became conscious of another sound. He did not begin to hear it all at once, he suddenly became aware that he had been hearing it all the time, a sound so much beyond all his experience and his powers of assimilation that up to this point he had been as oblivious of it as an ant or a flea might be of the sound of the avalanche on which it rides; he had been travelling upon water since early afternoon and for seven years now he had run his plow and harrow and planter within the very shadow of the levee on which he now stood, but this profound deep whisper which came from the further side of it he did not at once recognise. He stopped. The line of convicts behind jolted into him like a line of freight cars stopping, with an iron clashing like cars. "Get on!" a guard shouted.

"What's that?" the convict said. A negro man squatting before the nearest fire answered him:

"Dat's him. Dat's de Ole Man."

WILLIAM FAULKNER, *THE OLD MAN*

Preservation Hall performer, New Orleans, Louisiana

THEY FINISHED EATING. Then it began to rain again, as upon a signal, while they stood or squatted in their harsh garments which had not dried out during the night but had merely become slightly warmer than the air. Presently they were haled to their feet and told off into two groups, one of which was armed from a stack of mud-clogged picks and shovels nearby, and marched away up the levee. A little later the motor launch with its train of skiffs came up across what was, fifteen feet beneath its keel, probably a cotton field, the skiffs loaded to the gunwales with Negroes and a scattering of white people nursing bundles on their laps. When the engine shut off the faint plinking of a guitar came across the water. The skiffs warped in and unloaded; the convicts watched the men and women and children struggle up the muddy slope, carrying heavy towsacks and bundles wrapped in quilts. The sound of the guitar had not ceased and now the convicts saw him—a young, black, lean-hipped man, the guitar slung by a piece of cotton plowline about his neck. He mounted the levee, still picking it. He carried nothing else, no food, no change of clothes, not even a coat.

WILLIAM FAULKNER, *THE OLD MAN*

"Chopping cotton," Beulah, Mississippi

HE (THE OLD MAN) had recovered from his debauch, back in banks again, the Old Man, rippling placidly toward the sea, brown and rich as chocolate between levees whose inner faces were wrinkled as though in a frozen and aghast amazement, crowned with the rich green of summer in the willows; beyond them, sixty feet below, slick mules squatted against the broad pull of middle-busters in the richened soil which would not need to be planted, which would need only to be shown a cotton seed to sprout and make; there would be the symmetric miles of strong stalks by July, purple bloom in August, in September the black fields snowed over, spilled, the middles dragged smooth by the long sacks, the long black limber hands plucking, the hot air filled with the whine of gins....

WILLIAM FAULKNER, *THE OLD MAN*

Cotton-gin worker, Memphis, Tennessee

Porters at cotton factor's, Memphis

Boathouses, Red Wing, Minnesota

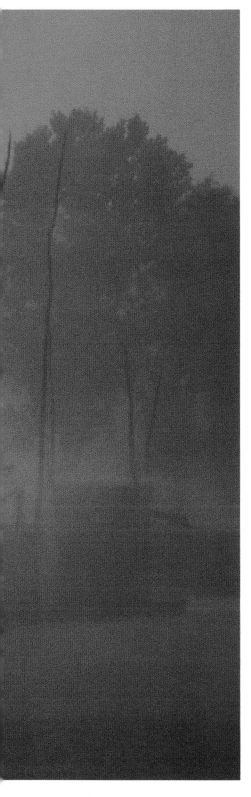

IT IS A LAZY LIFE, the life of the shantyboat fisherman. There is much time to talk. And there are few who are better conversationalists, with their mellow philosophy and vast store of information, so much of it inaccurate. I know of nothing more delightful than to sit in a flatboat while Catfish Johnny runs his lines, and listen to him tell of the lore of the river: how if you take a fish out of the Red River or Black River and drop it in Mississippi water it will die as quickly as though you had pierced it with a bullet; how fish will spoil quicker in the moonlight than under the sun. He will tell you how it is useless to fish after a night of bright moonlight, because fish will gorge themselves feeding in the light of the moon, and so the next day will bite at nothing; or how a fish cannot be kept with its head down stream or it will drown like a human. He will explain how if you wish to catch an alligator, you must put a piece of garlic on a stick, and when you poke this into the alligator's hole, the smell will drive him out in panic; he will describe how the fish travel on great highways through the water, just as if they were on roads marked out by Government men.

BEN LUCIEN BURMAN, *BIG RIVER TO CROSS*

Lake Wapanocca fisherman, Turrell, Arkansas

Band bus, New Orleans, Louisiana

SOME MONTHS AGO I went to see a panorama of the Rhine. It was like a dream of the Middle Ages. I floated down its historic stream in something more than imagination, under bridges built by the Romans, and repaired by later heroes, past cities and castles whose very names were music to my ears, and each of which was the subject of a legend. There were Ehrenbreitstein and Rolandseck and Coblentz, which I knew only in history. They were ruins that interested me chiefly. There seemed to come up from its waters and its vine-clad hills and valleys a hushed music as of Crusaders departing for the Holy Land. I floated along under the spell of enchantment, as if I had been transported to an heroic age, and breathed an atmosphere of chivalry.

Soon after, I went to see a panorama of the Mississippi, and as I worked my way up the river in the light of to-day, and saw the steamboats wooding up, counted the rising cities, gazed on the fresh ruins of Nauvoo, beheld the Indians moving west across the stream and, as before I had looked up the Moselle now looked up the Ohio and the Missouri and heard the legends of Dubuque and of Wenona's Cliff,—still thinking more of the future than of the past or present,—I saw that this was a Rhine stream of a different kind; that the foundations of castles were yet to be laid, and the famous bridges were yet to be thrown over the river; and I felt that *this was the heroic age itself,* though we know it not, for the hero is commonly the simplest and obscurest of men.

HENRY DAVID THOREAU, *WALKING*

Lansing, Iowa

Church congregation, Beulah, Mississippi

THE PEOPLE OF THE DELTA fear God and the Mississippi River. On Sunday mornings the air of the little towns vibrates with the ringing of church bells as the faithful of many sects and both races gather for worship. And in the springtime when the waters of the river are high against the levees, the faithful go, after services, to look at the yellow flood and ponder the possibilities of disaster. Its roaring can be heard in the Sabbath stillness of the streets, and steamboats on the swollen stream pass high above the level of the earth like monstrous birds in slow flight. It is then that the devout turn to God with prayers of supplication against the devouring Mississippi. It is to Him that thanks are given when at long last it flows safely on to the sea. And it is in His bosom that they nestle for comfort when they are engulfed by its waters.

DAVID COHN, *WHERE I WAS BORN AND RAISED*

Ruins of "Windsor," Port Gibson, Mississippi

(Pages 88-89, overleaf) "Houmas House," Burnside, Louisiana

HE IS GONE, with his family and his splendor. His broad acres are parcelled out in small shiftless farms which the jungle is taking again, and all that remains of him is the riverbed which he straightened out to keep his land from overflowing in the spring and the skeleton of a huge colonial house which neighbors have been pulling down piecemeal for fifty years and burning it a plank at a time for firewood, amid its grove of oaks.

But the Frenchman himself is forgotten, and his pride is now but a legend upon the land he had wrested from the earth and tamed and made fruitful: a monument to himself against the time when sleep should come upon his eyelids and depart not from them again; a legend which no longer has anything to do with the man even. The man is gone, his dream and his pride are dust with the lost dust of his anonymous bones, and in its place but the stubborn legend of the gold he buried when Grant swept through the land on his way to Chickamauga.

WILLIAM FAULKNER, *FATHER ABRAHAM*

AND STILL THERE IS NO SOUND in the world so filled with mystery and longing and unease as the sound at night of a river-boat blowing for the landing—one long, two shorts, one long, two shorts. Over the somber levels of the water pours that great voice, so long prolonged it is joined by echoes from the willowed shore, a chorus of ghosts, and, roused from sleep, wide-eyed and still, you are oppressed by vanished glories, the last trump, the calling of the ends of the earth, the current, cease-lessly moving out into the dark, of the eternal dying.

WILLIAM A. PERCY, *LANTERNS ON THE LEVEE*

Parlor in "Wigwam," Natchez, Mississippi

(Above and facing) Wedding party, Garden District, New Orleans, Louisiana

THE NICKNAME OF THE TRAIN was the Yellow Dog. Its real name was the Yazoo-Delta. It was a mixed train. The day was the 10th of September, 1923—afternoon. Laura McRaven, who was nine years old, was on her first journey alone. She was going up from Jackson to visit her mother's people, the Fairchilds, at their plantation named Shellmound, at Fairchilds, Mississippi. When she got there, "Poor Laura, little motherless girl," they would all run out and say, for her mother had died in the winter and they had not seen Laura since the funeral. Her father had come as far as Yazoo City with her and put her on the Dog. Her cousin Dabney Fairchild, who was seventeen, was going to be married, but Laura could not be in the wedding for the reason that her mother was dead. Of these facts the one most persistent in Laura's mind was the most intimate one: that her age was nine.

EUDORA WELTY, *DELTA WEDDING*

"Dunleith," Natchez, Mississippi

Garden party, Garden District, New Orleans

NO PLACE ON THIS PLANET could be half as fascinating as the plantation that I remember so well. It was a glamorous place, and even now, looking back across the years, I cannot see it stripped of its romantic quality. The house was large, white, and cool-looking. There were faded green window-blinds. A wide gallery stretched across the front of the building. Big red brick chimneys rose at the end of the gables. Vines grew riotously over everything. The house was set in a flower garden, and beyond the white palings of the fence there was a six-acre "front yard" in which sheep were kept, in order that the grass might always be smooth and short. On each side of the yard the sugar-cane fields stretched out to infinity. An avenue of pecan-trees led from the flower garden a quarter of a mile to the front gate. Before the gate was the road, then the levee, and beyond—the Mississippi River.

In ordinary times the levee presented a high green wall, a man-made mountain upon which cows and horses grazed. But in the spring, when the high water came, the river stood at the very top of the embankment, and from the front gallery of the plantation-house we could see the Mississippi River steamboats passing by, high in the air.

The river brought everything to us, and took everything away. All our supplies for the house came from the steamboats; and in the fall the cotton and sugar were loaded aboard and carried to New Orleans. The river was our one means of transportation—except for horses and carriages, of course—and the river and things pertaining to it furnished the topic for nearly all of our conversation.

LYLE SAXON, *FATHER MISSISSIPPI*

MY COUNTRY IS THE MISSISSIPPI DELTA, the river country. It lies flat, like a badly drawn half oval, with Memphis at its northern and Vicksburg at its southern tip. Its western boundary is the Mississippi River, which coils and returns on itself in great loops and crescents, though from the map you would think it ran in a straight line north and south. Every few years it rises like a monster from its bed and pushes over its banks to vex and sweeten the land it has made. For our soil, very dark brown, creamy and sweet-smelling, without substrata of rock or shale, was built up slowly, century after century, by the sediment gathered by the river in its solemn task of cleansing the continent and deposited in annual layers of silt on what must once have been the vast depression between itself and the hills. This ancient depression, now filled in and level, is what we call the Delta. Some say it was the floor of the sea itself. Now it seems still to be a floor, being smooth from one end to the other, without rise or dip or hill, unless the mysterious scattered monuments of the mound-builders may be called hills. The land does not drain into the river as most riparian lands do, but tilts back from it towards the hills of the south and east. Across this wide flat alluvial stretch—north and south it measures one hundred and ninety-six miles, east and west at the widest point fifty miles—run slowly and circuitously other rivers and creeks, also high-banked, with names pleasant to remember—Rattlesnake Bayou, Quiver River, the Bogue Phalia, the Tallahatchie, the Sunflower—pouring their tawny waters finally into the Yazoo, which in turn loses itself just above Vicksburg in the river. With us when you speak of "the river," though there are many, you mean always the same one, the great river, the shifting unappeasable god of the country, feared and loved, the Mississippi.

WILLIAM A. PERCY, *LANTERNS ON THE LEVEE*

Lake Maurepas, Louisiana

(Pages 98-99, overleaf) Marsh and canals south of New Orleans, Louisiana

Bayou, Louisiana

THERE WERE LONG OPENINGS, now and then, to right and left, of emerald-green savannah, with the dazzling blue of the Gulf far beyond, waving a thousand white handed good-byes as the funereal swamps slowly shut out again the horizon. How sweet the soft breezes off the moist prairies! How weird, how very near, the crimson and green and black and yellow sunsets! How dream-like the land and the great, whispering river! The profound stillness and breadth reminded the old German, so he said, of that early time when the evenings and mornings were the first days of the half-built world.

GEORGE WASHINGTON CABLE, *THE GRANDISSIMES*

Duck decoys, Reelfoot Lake, Tennessee

THIS DAY JANUARY 1ST 1821. *I am on Board a Keel Boat going down to New Orleans the poorest Man on it—*& What I have seen and felt has brought some very dearly purchased Experience, and Yet Yesterday I forgot that No servant could do for Me What I might do Myself; had I acted accordingly; My Port Folio Would now have been safe in my possession—

The Lands are flatening fast—the Orange trees are now and then seen near the Rich Planter's habitation—and the Verdure along all the shore is very Luxuriant and agreeable. At half past 6 o'clock P.M. we came opposite *Baton Rouge* but the Steam Boat had left and of Course we proceeded on our Way floating—this Last place is a Thrifty Villege on the New Orleans State—from some distance above Levees have made their appearance—I saw a Negro Man fishing by deeping a Scoup Net every moment in the Watter immediately at a point Where the current ran swift forming an eddy below, he had taken several tolerably Large Cat Fishes—

JOHN JAMES AUDUBON, *FROM HIS JOURNALS*

Fishing in flooded soybean field, Greenwood, Mississippi

Boathouses, Red Wing, Minnesota

(Above and facing) Sulphur mining, Port Sulphur, Louisiana

THE TWENTIETH CENTURY COMMERCE is a movement not of steamers but of barges, not of passengers but of freight. The splendor of the steamboats is replaced by a plodding business in grain and gravel, oil and fertilizer, steel and stone. There are no races down the river, no music and dancing, no crowds waiting at the levees. But it is a vastly more important commerce than was carried by the fleets that once lined the river front at St. Louis and St. Paul.

WALTER HAVIGHURST, *UPPER MISSISSIPPI*

Pilottown, Louisiana

WHEN YOU COME TO CONSIDER IT, there should be more collisions than there are on the river. Especially on some of the smaller tributaries, the bends are so sharp that there is no way to see around them; and the hills go up on both sides, hiding any trace of smoke that may warn a pilot of another tow. You might hear the other fellow's whistle, and then again you might not. It depends on the wind and the noises on your own boat. And so there you are, going downstream sticking that enormous snout of your tow out ahead of you across a point you can't see around. You'll be going slow, backing, probably. But you can't stop and you know it. It's just about impossible to stop a big tow going downstream, except by getting lines ashore and checking against some large trees. That takes a long time, and the big trees aren't always handy. And if you do find some of them, in high water when the current is strong, a heavy tow may snap a couple of hefty trees as if they were matchsticks. The boat will be backing full ahead. There might be a sharp report first, like that of a gun going off. That'll be one of the two-inch hawsers breaking as a thread breaks. A rope end will whip around, and you'll be lucky if none of your men is in the way of it; because it will shatter his leg or cut it off, sure. And then there'll be a cracking in the woods and a rustle in the leaves. And the men who have been making the shore tie will run, looking behind them and up, with afraid faces. Then the trees will come over, both of them at once, slowly at first, and then fast, and you'll be fortunate if they don't fall across your tow or on your boat. And you'll still be going down the river, with your boat backing full head, dragging a couple of big trees alongside in the water. If you meet another tow at that point it won't be funny, not funny at all.

EDWIN AND LOUISE ROSSKAM, *TOWBOAT RIVER*

Repairing rope, barge deck

(Pages 110-111, overleaf) New Orleans, Louisiana

French Quarter, New Orleans

(Pages 114-115, overleaf) Mardi Gras, New Orleans

[JANUARY, 1819] NEW ORLEANS HAS, at first sight, a very imposing and handsome appearance, beyond any other city in the United States in which I have yet been. The strange and loud noise heard through the fog, on board the *Clio,* proceeding from the voices of the market people and their customers, was not more extraordinary than the appearance of these noisy folk when the fog cleared away and we landed. Everything had an odd look. For twenty-five years I have been a traveler only between New York and Richmond, and I confess that I felt myself in some degree again a cockney, for it was impossible not to stare at a sight wholly new even to one who has traveled much in Europe and America.

BENJAMIN H. LATROBE, FROM HIS JOURNAL

(Facing, above, and pages 118-119, overleaf) Mardi Gras, New Orleans

[NEW ORLEANS, 1846] It was quite a novelty and a refreshing sight to see a whole population giving up their minds for a short season to amusement. There was a grand procession parading the streets, almost every one dressed in the most grotesque attire, troops of them on horseback, some in open carriages, with bands of music, and in a variety of costumes—some as Indians, with feathers in their heads, and one, a jolly fat man, as Mardi Gras himself. All wore masks, and here and there in the crowd, or stationed in a balcony above, we saw persons armed with bags of flour, which they showered down copiously on any one who seemed particularly proud of his attire.

CHARLES LYELL, *A SECOND VISIT TO THE UNITED STATES OF NORTH AMERICA*

WHEN POWERHOUSE first came back from intermission, no doubt full of beer, they said, he got the band tuned up again in his own way. He didn't strike the piano keys for pitch—he simply opened his mouth and gave falsetto howls—in A, D and so on—they tuned by him. Then he took hold of the piano, as if he saw it for the first time in his life, and tested it for strength, hit it down in the bass, played an octave with his elbow, lifted the top, looked inside, and leaned against it with all his might. He sat down and played it for a few minutes with outrageous force and got it under his power—a bass deep and coarse as a sea net —then produced something glimmering and fragile, and smiled. And who could ever remember any of the things he says? They are just inspired remarks that roll out of his mouth like smoke.

EUDORA WELTY, *POWERHOUSE*

Preservation Hall, New Orleans

Crayfish, New Orleans

Fishing boats at dock

MY FIRST BOON-COMPANION WAS SKILLET, the small dark son of Mère's cook. He was the best crawfisher in the world and I was next. Instead of closed sewers our town had open ditches, which after an overflow swarmed with crawfish, small clear ones, quite shrimp-like, whose unexpected backward agility saved them from any except the most skilful hands, and large red ones, surly and whiskered, with a startling resemblance to the red-nosed old reprobates you saw around the saloons when you were looking for tobacco tags in the sawdust. When these rared back and held their claws wide apart, Skillet said they were saying: "Swear to God, white folks, I ain't got no tail." Theoretically it was for their tails that we hunted them, because when boiled and seasoned and prayed over they made that thick miraculous pink soup you never experience unless you have French blood in the family or unless you dine at Prunier's.

WILLIAM A. PERCY, *LANTERNS ON THE LEVEE*

AFTER A WHILE, when we had had our last look at New Orleans, I found myself a nice corner up on the top deck right under the pilot house and settled down with my trumpet and a polishing rag. I had bought myself a fine new instrument just before starting out, but even that wasn't shiny enough for *this* trip. No, suh! So I took the rag and shined her a little and then I put her to my mouth and tried out a few blasts. She sounded strong and sweet, with a good pure tone. I swung a little tune and saw we were going to get along fine together. So then I rubbed her up some more, taking my time, until I was satisfied. Over on the left shore a great cypress swamp was passing slowly by—there must have been hundreds of miles of it, stretching away off to the west—dark and hung all over with Spanish moss. I felt very happy where I was. The sun was just warm enough, the chunking of the paddle wheels was now pleasant to hear and everything was peaceful. Pretty soon I spread the rag on the deck beside me and lay my new trumpet on it and began to think of how lucky I really was. There I was, only nineteen years old, a member of a fine band, and starting out on my first big adventure. And I had my new trumpet to take with me. I reached over and let my hand lay on it, and felt very comfortable....

LOUIS ARMSTRONG, *SWING THAT MUSIC*

French Quarter, New Orleans

(Pages 126-127, overleaf) Oil platforms, Gulf of Mexico

Paddlewheel, <u>Mississippi Queen</u>